D1530768

C   5255

FUN WITH SCIENCE

WEATHER

STEVE PARKER

Contents

Use the symbols below to help you
identify the three kinds of practical
activities in this book.

EXPERIMENTS

TRICKS

THINGS TO MAKE

Illustrated by Kuo Kang Chen · Peter Bull

WARWICK PRESS

Introduction

Have you noticed the weather today? Is it bright and sunny, or cloudy and overcast, or dull and raining? Hot, warm, cool, or cold? Or have you been indoors, and not noticed the weather for a few hours.

The first part of this book tells you about the features of our ever-changing weather, such as temperature, winds, clouds, and storms. The middle part shows how weather is measured, and how weather forecasts are made. The last part looks at how the weather affects us—and how we might be affecting the weather.

Throughout the book, there are simple and safe experiments, projects and tricks which you can carry out. The questions on these two pages are based on the scientific ideas explained in this book. As you carry out the experiments, you should be able to answer these questions, and understand more about the weather and how it affects the world around us.

This book covers six main topics:

- Atmosphere, air, temperature, and wind
- Days and seasons, winds, and water currents around the globe
- Moisture in the air, humidity, clouds, rain, snow, and hail
- Thunder and lightning, rainbows, and mirages
- Weather forecasts and weather maps
- How the weather shapes the land and affects animals, plants, and people

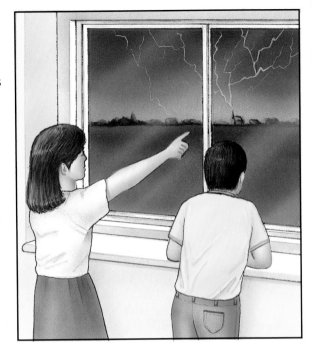

▲ How far away is a thunderstorm? (pages 24–25)

▼ What are "all the colors of the rainbow," and how can you make them for yourself? (page 26)

▼ How does the weather help us to design our homes and buildings? (page 35)

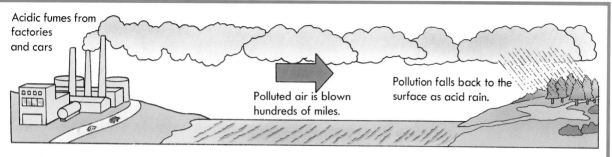

Acidic fumes from factories and cars

Polluted air is blown hundreds of miles.

Pollution falls back to the surface as acid rain.

▲ Are we changing the weather? How will this affect our world? (pages 38–39)

► What is wind, and how do we measure it? (pages 10–15)

▼ What is temperature? How can we tell how hot or cold it is? (pages 6–9)

▲ How do experts predict the weather? And how often are they right? (pages 28–31)

◄ How does the Earth's place in space make day and night? (page 8)

▼ Where does rain come from, and how can you tell the amount that falls? (pages 16–21)

► How does the climate affect where plants and animals live? (pages 34–37)

An Ocean of Air

It is all around us, but cannot be seen. We can only feel it when it blows on our faces. We can only hear it as it rustles the trees and whistles past buildings. Yet we need to breathe it, or we will die. It is air. Our world is covered with air, called the **atmosphere**. The Earth's gravity keeps it near its surface. Otherwise our spinning planet would fling it off into space.

The Atmosphere

The air in our atmosphere is made of a mixture of colorless gases. These are mainly nitrogen (almost four-fifths), oxygen (one-fifth), plus many other gases, such as argon and carbon dioxide, in tiny amounts.

The air in the atmosphere is densest, or "thickest,'" near the ground. As we travel higher it becomes thinner, or more rarefied.

You can feel the weight of air by spreading a large sheet of newspaper flat on a table, and sliding a ruler under one side, as shown below. Hit the ruler hard. It is difficult to lift the paper, because of the weight of air pressing on it. This is called air pressure, and it pushes down at about 14 pounds per square inch.

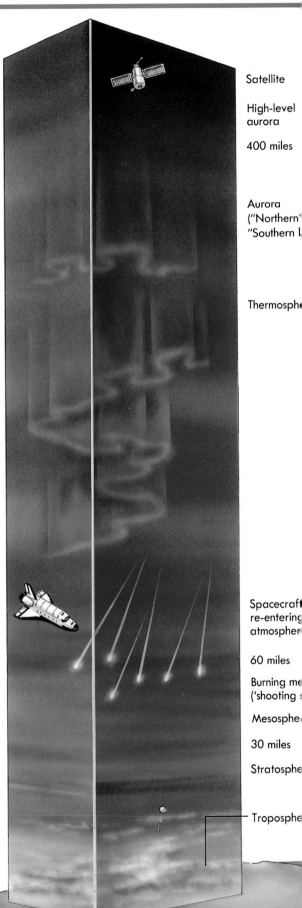

Satellite

High-level aurora

400 miles

Aurora ("Northern "Southern L

Thermosph

Spacecraf re-entering atmospher

60 miles

Burning me ('shooting

Mesosphe

30 miles

Stratosphe

Troposphe

Paper

Thump ruler with your fist.

Using Air to Hold up Water

Air presses in all directions as this trick shows. Fill a clean beaker to the brim with water. Press a square piece of strong cardboard on top to make a good seal. Keeping the beaker over the sink, very carefully turn it over . . . and the water should stay inside!

Air pushes upward on cardboard and keeps water in.

Air is pressing upward on the cardboard with enough force to hold the water in place. Push down gently on the corner of the cardboard to break the seal, and air bubbles in it. It now presses downward as well as up. The cardboard falls away, and the water pours out.

Balancing Balloons!

Air, like most substances, becomes bigger (**expands**) as it is heated. Show that a certain volume of hot air weighs less than the same volume of cold air, by a '''balloon balance.''' Blow up two balloons to the same size. Tie each balloon to one end of a long, thin piece of wood (such as a dowel or garden cane). Balance this on a pencil supported by cans or books, and mark the balance point on the wood.

Tip: The balloons are the same size when they touch the pot's side.

Pot

Balloon

Next, put one balloon in a cold place such as the refrigerator, and the other in a warm place. Let some air out of the warm balloon and blow some air into the cold balloon, so that they are the same size. Now do they balance?

Balloon with warm air

Balloon with cold air

Testing the Temperature

Air temperature is the '"hotness"' or "coldness"' of the air. This is measured by an instrument known as a thermometer. Warmth in the air spreads to warm the substance inside the thermometer. This expands as it heats up. A scale on the thermometer shows the temperature, which is usually measured in degrees Fahrenheit, written °F. Weather experts use different types of thermometers for different jobs.

Mercury thermometer

Alcohol thermometer

Maximum-minimum thermometer

Liquid-crystal thermometer

▲ A Campbell-Stokes sunshine recorder. The Sun's rays burn a line on a paper chart. Its length shows hours of sunlight.

◄ An alcohol thermometer is used in very cold places, as the usual mercury freezes at minus 38°F.

In the summer
You can record air temperatures with a thermometer on a shady wall, out of direct sunlight. The temperature on a hot summer day is 75–90°F.

In the winter
In winter the average temperatures are much lower. Water freezes at 32°F. When the air temperature falls below this for a time, ponds and lakes ice over.

Heat from the Sun

The Sun gives out rays of various types. We can see one type—these are light rays, or sunlight. The Sun also gives out heat, in the form of infrared rays.

Smooth, shiny surfaces reflect both light and heat rays. Dull, roughened surfaces absorb them. A simple experiment reveals the power of the Sun to warm different substances by different amounts.

Water

Thermometer

Soil

On windowsill in Sun

Out of Sun

Thermometer

Water

Soil

Black cloth

▲ In hot places, people wear loose, light-colored clothes. The light color reflects the Sun's heat, keeping the person cool.

You need two identical glass jars. Carefully half-fill one with dark, fairly dry soil and the other with water. Put them on a sunny windowsill (above left), and measure their temperatures straight away with a standard mercury thermometer. (Take extra care, mercury is poisonous.)

Measure their temperatures again after half an hour and one hour. The dark soil absorbs the Sun's heat more quickly than the '''shiny''' water and so warms up more rapidly. Now place both jars in a shady place indoors, under a dark cloth (below left). Which one cools down more quickly?

Where's Warmest and Coldest

The world's hottest place is Dallol, Ethiopia. Average temperatures over several years were 94°F. Coldest is on Antarctica, where the average temperatures are minus 70°F!

Days and Seasons

Planet Earth's movements in space produce the regular changes of day and night, and summer and winter. The planets circle a star, which we call the Sun. It takes one year for the Earth to make a complete circuit. The Earth also spins around itself, once each day.

Summer and Winter, Day and Night

The Earth is not at right angles to the Sun. It is tilted slightly. On its yearly journey around the Sun, the upper part of the Earth (the North) is nearer to the Sun for a few months. The Sun's rays pass almost straight down through the atmosphere, so less of their energy is lost in the atmosphere, and more reaches the surface. It is summer in the North.

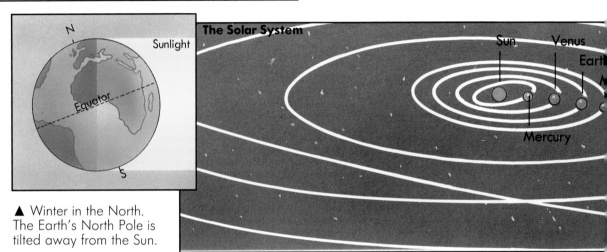

The Solar System

Sun   Venus   Earth

Mercury

▲ Winter in the North. The Earth's North Pole is tilted away from the Sun.

Make a Garden Sundial

You can use the Sun to tell the time, by making a sundial, as shown on the right. Cover a board or large book with white paper for a base. Make a right-angled triangle of cardboard about 6 inches long at the base, with a flap at the bottom. Stick the flap on the base, using thread guy ropes if necessary to keep it upright. Draw two curved lines from the corners of the base to the triangle's high side.

Place the sundial where it will get the Sun for most of the day. Use a compass to make the tall vertical side of the triangle point north. Through the day, as the Sun moves it casts a shadow from the cardboard. With a watch to tell the time, mark and label the shadow's position each hour, where it crosses the curved lines. Next day, you can use the sundial to tell the time—provided it is sunny!

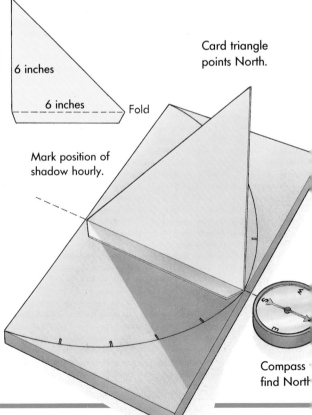

6 inches

6 inches   Fold

Card triangle points North.

Mark position of shadow hourly.

Compass find North

Table-tennis ball "globe"

Flashlight

Pin

Meanwhile, the lower part of the Earth (the South) is farther from the Sun. The rays pass at a slanting angle through the atmosphere, where much of their energy is absorbed. It is winter in the South. As the Earth reaches the opposite side of its circle around the Sun, the seasons are reversed.

Draw a simple world map on a table-tennis ball. Carefully stick this on a pin, and shine a narrow-beam flashlight from the side. Twirl the ball slowly to show how day and night happen. Can you see why, on Earth, the Sun seems to travel across the sky?

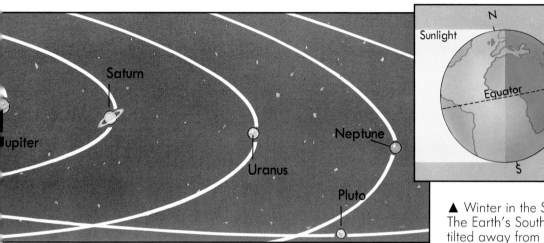

Saturn

Jupiter

Uranus

Neptune

Pluto

N

Sunlight

Equator

S

▲ Winter in the South. The Earth's South Pole is tilted away from the Sun.

▶ The Sun's light and heat rays are a powerful source of energy. Solar panels capture this energy and turn it into electricity. The car *Sunraycer* won a race across Australia, powered only by the Sun. Solar power will be important in the future, since it causes little pollution and the Sun will last for billions of years.

Where's the Hottest?

The highest temperature ever recorded was in Libya. The temperature was 136°F. And that was in the shade, which is the standard way to read the air temperature. In the sun it was hotter!

Measuring the Way the Wind Blows

When we say '''a north wind''' we refer to the direction the wind blows from, not where it blows to. You can make a wind recorder (*right*) to measure the wind's direction.

Put a length of dowel through two thread spools so that it spins easily. Glue one reel onto the base of a shoebox, the other on the lid directly above, with a hole in the lid for the dowel. Tape a piece of paper to the lid, for the recording chart. Make a wind vane from a triangle of cardboard, and fix a soft-lead pencil (6B) to its upright edge. Tape the middle of the vane to the dowel, so that as it spins the pencil draws a line on the recording chart. Place the wind recorder in an exposed place, steadied by stones in the shoebox. Draw a North–South line on the recording chart. As the wind changes direction, the pencil traces a line on the chart. The thickest part of the line shows where the wind has been blowing from for most of the time.

Equipment: Shoebox, two thread spools, about 14 inches of dowel to fit in the reels, compass, 6B pencil, paper, glue, triangle of strong cardboard, sticky tape.

Cardboard wind-vane taped to dowel.

Soft-leaded pencil taped to wind-vane.

Thread spool glued to box lid.

New paper recording chart for each day

Thin dowel through thread spools

Compass to indicate North-South.

Shoebox

Thread spool glued to box base.

The World's Winds

The Sun's heat energy warms different parts of the atmosphere by day and by night, and through the seasons. This keeps our weather on the move. Warm air is lighter than cold air and rises (*see page 5*). Cold air flows in to take its place. These movements create large-scale wind patterns or "wind belts'" around the world.

There are Polar Easterlies, Trades, and Prevailing Westerlies. Along the Equator is a region where winds seldom blow, the Doldrums.

North Polar Easterly

North Prevailing Westerly

North Trade

Doldrums

South Trade

South Polar Easterly

South Prevailing Westerly

Water—Warm and Cold

Just as the Sun warms the atmosphere and creates winds, so it warms the surface of the oceans and helps to create water currents. You can demonstrate that cold water is heavier, or more dense, than warm water in your own bathtub!

Put a few drops of food coloring in a plastic bottle. Fill this with cold water and shake it to color the water evenly. Screw on the top and place the bottle in the refrigerator for a few hours, so that the water becomes even colder. Half fill the bathtub with warm water. Place the plastic bottle on the bottom. Carefully unscrew the top so that the cold, colored water seeps out slowly. Watch how this cold, dense water spreads out—but stays near the bottom of the bath.

Plastic bottle of very cold water

Food coloring

Warm water in bathtub

The World's Currents

The Sun's warmth and the winds, plus the spinning of the Earth, the tidal pull of the Moon and Sun combine to create oceanic water currents. The currents also change direction to flow around the great land masses.

These currents affect our weather, and they carry vast amounts of water. The West Wind Drift, which flows westward around Antarctica, transports more than 200 times the amount of water carried by the Amazon.

Warm-water currents (red)   Cold-water currents (blue)

Power from the Wind

We can capture the Sun's energy directly, as light and/or heat (*solar power, see page 9*). We can also capture it indirectly from the weather, by harnessing the power of the winds it creates. Like solar power, wind power produces little pollution, and it will be available as long as the Sun itself lasts.

Some people say that rows of huge windmills are a form of "visual pollution."

To make a windmill, carefully cut four vanes in a star shape from stiff cardboard, as shown below. Fold back a strip along one edge, on the same side, of each vane. Fix the star to a piece of dowel or cane, with a thumbtack through its center, so that it is free to turn. Hold the windmill facing into a good stiff breeze, and it should spin rapidly. What happens if you fold the strips on each vane forward instead of backward?

▲▼ Windmills have been used for centuries (*above*), to grind wheat into flour, pump water, and do other tasks. The modern version (*below*) converts wind power into electricity.

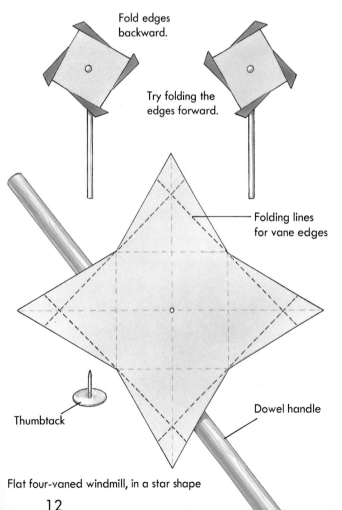

Fold edges backward.

Try folding the edges forward.

Folding lines for vane edges

Thumbtack

Dowel handle

Flat four-vaned windmill, in a star shape

Put a Sock in the Wind!

Windsocks are used at airports, seaports, and other exposed places such as mountain roads (*right*). The sock swivels away from the wind, which then blows into its open end or "mouth.'" The sock's tail points the way the wind is blowing. A stiff sock means a strong wind. If it flops loosely, the wind is only light. You can make a windsock using the instructions below.

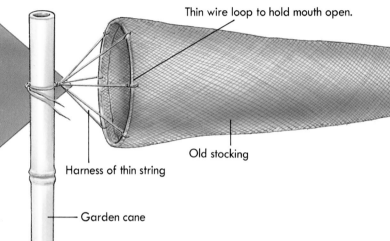

Thin wire loop to hold mouth open.

Old stocking

Harness of thin string

Garden cane

Where is Windiest Place?

The strongest wind was 230 miles per hour on Mount Washington, New Hampshire.

In the United States, wind speeds are given in miles per hour. In most other countries they are given in kilometers per hour.

Bubbles Blowing in the Wind

Equipment: Bubble-blowing kit.
Care: No bubbles near busy roads!

Most winds blow in one direction. On a local scale, this can vary with features such as hills, trees, and buildings, that make the wind change direction and slow down or speed up. Reveal local wind patterns by blowing bubbles outside on a windy day. Watch them go around or over obstacles.

The Devastating Hurricane

A hurricane is formed when strong winds blow into an area of low air pressure (*see page 30*), and swirl violently in a circle. They develop over the warm tropical waters of the Atlantic Ocean, in the summer. Similar storms are called cyclones in the Indian Ocean, and typhoons in the Pacific.

Hurricane hotspots

▲ Tropical storm hot-spots around the world. Where they hit the land, the strong winds do immense damage.

Hurricane

◀ Average wind speeds in a hurricane are at least 74 miles per hour. Yet in the '''eye''' at the center, there is hardly any wind at all.

▼ A satellite photograph of a hurricane over the Gulf of Mexico. The dashed lines show the coast. A computer has color-coded the scene, with the strongest winds in red.

How Fast is the Wind Blowing?

With the help of an adult, you can make an **anemometer** to measure how fast the wind blows, as shown here.

Bend a loop at the end of a length of stiff wire. File the other end flat. Tape the loop to the bottom of a shoebox. Put stones in the box to steady it, and place the lid on, making a hole for the wire. Tape two thin pieces of wood into a cross. Push four paper cups onto the ends of the wood, facing in a circle. Securely fix the center of the cross to the end (top) of an empty ballpoint pen tube with a

Equipment: Four paper cups, drawing pin, tape, pin, pen tube, two pieces of wood, wire, shoebox, cotton, clay.

thumbtack and sticky tape. Push a pin through the tiny hole in the side of the tube, and place it on the wire upright, so that it pivots easily on the pin. Now take the anemometer to a windy place outside, on a table. (*Continued below.*)

Thumbtack

Pin in ventilation hole on side of pen case

Wooden cross pieces taped and pinned to pen tube.

Hole in shoebox lid

Empty ballpoint pen tube

Wire upright

Shoebox

...thanger or similar wire, ...ped at bottom.

Loop taped into shoebox

Cotton thread

(*Continued from above.*) Tie a length of thread to the pin in the side of the tube, leading it sideways over a roller (the center of a kitchen roll). Let it hang down at the side of the table. Fix a small modeling clay weight at the end of the thread (*left*). Let the cups go, and they should swing around in the wind. Use a

watch to time how long the clay weight takes to rise from the ground to the edge of the table.

Repeat your experiment morning, midday, and evening, on several days, for different types of wind.

Moisture in the Air

The air in the atmosphere is hardly ever dry. It contains **water vapor**, which is the '''gas''' form of water. Like other atmospheric gases, water vapor is invisible. But when the vapor turns to liquid (**condenses**) it forms small floating droplets of water, which we see as clouds, mist, and fog. When the droplets become too big, they come down as rain.

Water dries quickly in sunshine.

Water dries more slowly in shade.

"Disappearing''' Water!

After a rainstorm, there are puddles everywhere. But when the Sun comes out, they soon disappear. Where does the water go? The Sun's warmth turns the liquid water into invisible water vapor, by **evaporation**. (Evaporation is the reverse of condensation.) The water '''dries up.''

Changing liquid water into vaporized water requires energy, usually in the form of heat. When our bodies get very hot, after much exercise, sweat droplets form on our skin. As the water in the droplets evaporates, it draws heat from the body and so we cool down.

You can show that the Sun's heat evaporates water by a simple experiment (*above*). Put two identical saucers on a sunny windowsill, and half-fill each with cold water. Put a '''sunshade''' over one, such as a propped-up book. Shielded from the Sun's rays, the water in this saucer dries less quickly than the water in full sunshine.

Where's Foggiest?

Fog and mist are tiny water droplets floating in the air, like clouds at ground level. In a true fog, it is impossible to see clearly for more than 1,000 yards. On the Grand Banks, off Canada's Newfoundland, it is sometimes foggy for weeks on end. Here, there are true fogs for an average of one day in three each year.

Evaporating sweat from the skin cools the body when we are too hot.

Humidity—Wet or Dry?

Standard thermometer with 'dry' bulb

Wet-bulb thermometer

Wet-bulb reading is lower than dry-bulb.

Wet muslin wrapped around bulb.

Bulb

The amount of water vapor in the air is called the humidity. When the humidity is low, sweat evaporates quickly from the body, and our skin feels dry. In high humidity, sweat cannot evaporate easily since the air already carries much water vapor. We say the weather is "muggy"' or '''sticky."

Humidity level is measured by a psychrometer. This is made from two thermometers: a standard dry-bulb one, and one with wet muslin wrapped around it. Water evaporates from the wet bulb, and so this one registers a lower temperature. The greater the difference between the two readings, the lower the humidity.

▶ A home-made psychrometer needs two thermometers. The wet bulb must be kept very damp all the time for an accurate reading.

Handy Hints for Desert Survival!

Water is continuously evaporating into the air from many places on the Earth's surface, including seas, lakes, rivers, damp soil, wet roofs, and roads, and plants and animals. This can be trapped as liquid water by a moisture trap, using the temperature change between day and night.

For people lost in the desert, this small drink could mean the difference between life and death. You do not have to be stranded in the desert, your own yard or park will do, provided you are allowed to dig a hole!

The Moisture Trap

Dig a conical hole and put in it a plastic beaker. In late afternoon, spread over it a plastic sheet, anchor it with large stones and place smaller pebbles in the center (right). Cool air holds less water vapor than warm air. As the temperature falls at night, water vapor in the air and from the soil condenses on the plastic sheet and drips into the beaker.

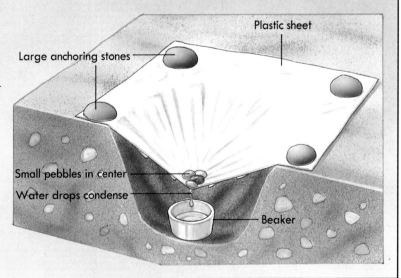

Plastic sheet

Large anchoring stones

Small pebbles in center

Water drops condense

Beaker

Clouding the View

One of the most obvious features of our weather are the clouds floating across the sky. They are made of billions of water droplets formed from condensed water vapor, or of ice crystals made from frozen water droplets.

There are several main types of cloud, according to their shape and their height above the Earth's surface. For example, cirrus clouds are thin, wispy "streams" at heights of over 6 miles. Cumulus clouds have flat bases and billowing, fluffy tops. Experts can predict the weather from the cloud types and the speed at which they move, blown by the wind. Cumulus may bring showers, while nimbostratus means long periods of rain.

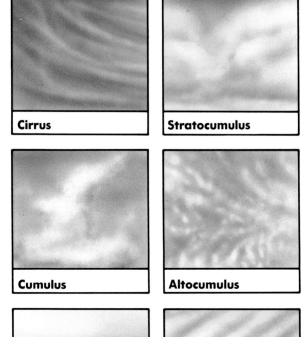

Cirrus

Stratocumulus

Cumulus

Altocumulus

Stratus

Nimbus

▲ "Smog" is a combination of smoke and fog. It forms where air is polluted with vehicle exhaust fumes. There is a complicated chemical reaction between the fumes and the air, in the presence of sunlight. This smog-bound city is Santiago, in Chile. Smog can be prevented if cars become cleaner.

► Towering cumulonimbus are often called "storm clouds." They tend to bring lightning, thunder, and heavy rain (see page 24). The dark base is only about half a mile above the ground. The anvil-shaped spreading top may be over 4 miles high.

Cumulonimbus

Clouds in the Bathroom?

Run a warm bath in a cold bathroom and the air soon turns steamy and "cloudy." The "steam" is a mixture of water vapor and tiny water droplets, like the ones that form clouds. It floats up in air which rises because it has been warmed by the hot water in the bathtub. Water vapor condenses on cold surfaces like the windows. These are like dewdrops, which condense from air onto the ground, when a cold night follows a warm day.

See "Invisible" Dust!

Air is hardly ever perfectly clean. Tiny particles of dust float on the slightest wind. This is important, because each water droplet or ice crystal, in a cloud or fog, needs a tiny particle around which it can form and grow. It may be a piece of solid matter from dust or smoke, or salt from seaspray, or even chemicals from vehicle exhausts and factory fumes. You can see the "invisible" dust in air by almost closing the curtains on a very sunny day. Tiny bits of dust glint in the narrow shafts of sunlight.

Particles of dust reflect sunlight.

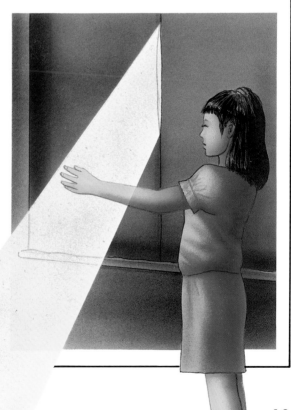

The Water Cycle

The Earth always has about the same amount of water. This water is always on the move, in a never-ending cycle. The water cycle produces the most noticeable parts of our weather—clouds, fog, rain, and snow.

Water vapor in the atmosphere condenses to form clouds and fog. Water falls to the surface as rain, and also frozen as hail and snow (see page 22). This "fallen water" travels around on the surface. It filters through the soil, and runs in streams and rivers to the sea. Meanwhile, water is passing from the surface back into the air, as it evaporates to form water vapor. This "risen water" also travels around in the atmosphere, carried as clouds and invisible water vapor blown by the wind.

▶ Water changes from vapor, to liquid, to solid and back again. The entire cycle is driven by heat energy from the Sun.

How Much Rain Have We Had?

You can record rainfall by making a simple rain gauge. Choose an open area such as a lawn, which is not shielded from the rain.

Bury a large jar with its neck at ground level. Carefully cut a small hole in the center of a square sheet of stiff plastic (like the plastic packaging around toys). Choose a plastic funnel with the same diameter as the jar, cutting its top down if necessary. Jam its spout into the hole and put the sheet over the jar (right).

Each day, lift out the jar and measure the depth of rain water inside. This is how much rain has fallen since the last reading. Always tip away the water before replacing the jar!

Plastic funnel

Stiff plastic sheet or card

Large jam jar

Rain water collects in jar

Where is Wettest?

Rainfall is measured in inches per year. The world's wettest place is Tutunendo, in Colombia, South America. It's average is 463 inches of rain each year! The average rainfall in New York City is a mere 44 inches.

SUN   Clouds   Rain

Evaporation from the sea

Evaporation from the soil

Evaporation from plants and animals

Evaporation from lakes and rivers

Flowing water in streams and rivers

Ground water filters through soil and rocks.

From Raindrops to Dry Puddles

Chalk line marks edge of puddle 1 hour ago.

Here are two simple experiments to study rain. Find an area where a puddle always forms after rain, such as on paving stones or tarmac. When the rain stops, draw a line around the puddle's edge with a piece of chalk. Then draw another line each hour afterward, to measure how fast the puddle dries out (*right*). Try the experiment in different kinds of weather. You can probably guess that the puddle will dry faster if the Sun shines. But what about wind? Does the puddle disappear faster on a calm day or a windy one?

You can also compare the number and size of raindrops. Carefully cut a large sheet of plain, absorbent paper, such as the back of a spare length of wallpaper. Put the paper out in light drizzle for a certain time, such as five seconds. Quickly draw around the wet spots caused by the raindrops (*below*). Compare the result with the spots from a heavy shower.

5 seconds in light drizzle

5 seconds in heavy shower

Rain, Hail, and Snow

Water moves from the atmosphere to the Earth's surface in many forms, including rain, hail, snow, frost, and dew. Sometimes the water goes straight back to the atmosphere. For example, a light snowfall may melt as soon as the Sun comes out, and the water evaporates back in the air. Or snow might fall in a very cold place, such as Antarctica, and be covered by more snow. Over time it is compressed into ice, and stays there for thousands of years. Both these journeys are part of the water cycle.

Raindrops usually form as ice crystals in a cloud, but they melt as they fall. Snowflakes form in the same way, but stay frozen if the air temperature is at or below freezing point, 32°F. Hailstones are raindrops that move back up into the cloud on rising air currents, and freeze into solid balls of ice.

Rain (air above freezing point)

Snow (air below freezing point)

Hail (drops carried upward and downward several times)

Height on mountain above which air temperature is below freezing point

Rain

Snow

Hail

Biggest Hailstones

Most hailstones are pea-sized, but occasionally are large. A huge hailstone fell on Kansas, in 1970. It measured 7 inches across and weighed more than 26 oz. Bigger ones have fallen, but no one has measured them before they melted!

Layer of snow acts as an insulating blanket

Be Jack Frost: Make a Pattern on a Plate!

At night, water vapor condenses from the air and normally forms dewdrops. If the surface temperature is below freezing, the water freezes into ice crystals, which we call frost.

To make a frost pattern smear a little makeup cream or petroleum jelly on your finger, and draw a design on a clean glass plate. Put the plate in a freezer next to a plastic beaker of warm water. The water vapor condenses and freezes on the clean parts of the plate, but not on the greasy parts. After an hour or two, your pattern is revealed!

After freezing

Snug under the Snow

Snow may feel icy to us but in very cold places, such as the Arctic, a covering of snow acts like a blanket that helps many creatures and plants to keep relatively warm. Above the snow, in the icy blasts of winter wind, the air temperature may fall to minus 40°F. or even lower. But the layer of loose snow holds tiny pockets of trapped air, just like a feather eiderdown. Air is a good insulator. Under their blanket of snow, creatures like lemmings and voles dig tunnels and continue to feed through the coldest weather. The temperature in the tunnels is only just below freezing—but that is much warmer than above the snow!

Lemmings dig tunnels at ground level under the snow.

Light and Sound

The weather can veer from one extreme to another in minutes. In a thunderstorm, deafening claps of thunder shake the ground and bolts of lightning split the dark sky. This is weather at its most powerful and violent. Yet soon after, the thunderclouds roll away, the wind drops, the Sun comes out, and a rainbow arches across the sky.

Make Your Own Lightning!

Equipment: A large iron or steel pot (not aluminum) with a plastic handle, a rubber glove, an iron or steel fork, and a plastic sheet.

You can make a tiny, harmless version of a lightning flash at home. Tape a plastic sheet to a table top. Hold a large iron pan by its insulating handle, with a rubber glove on that hand, and rub the pan vigorously to and fro on the plastic sheet. This gives the pan an electrical charge (see opposite). Then, holding

▲ The cactus desert of Arizona is lit up by jagged bolts of lightning known as "fork lightning." If the flash is far away, or spread out through the clouds, it is "sheet lightning."

a fork firmly in the other hand, bring its prongs slowly near to the pan's rim. When the gap between pan and fork is small, a tiny spark should jump across. (It may help to darken the room by drawing the curtains, to see the spark more clearly.) It is as though the pan is the "thundercloud," the fork is the "lightning conductor" (see opposite), and you are the "Earth's surface."

Rubber glove

Large iron or steel pan

Sparks jumps across gap

Iron or steel fork

Plastic sheet

How Far Away is Thunder?

In a thundercloud, small ice crystals, with positive electrical charges, float up near the top of the cloud. Larger ones, with negative charges, stay near the bottom. This separation of electrical charges is very unstable, and lightning is the way the charges are equalized again. The first part of the flash, the "lead stroke," carries negative electricity down toward the ground. It is met by the "return stroke" bringing positive charges up from the ground. The intensely hot lightning bolt heats the air around it, which suddenly expands, making the noise of thunder.

► Lightning and thunder are created together, but light travels faster than sound. Count the seconds between flash and clap, divide by 5. This is the storm's distance in miles.

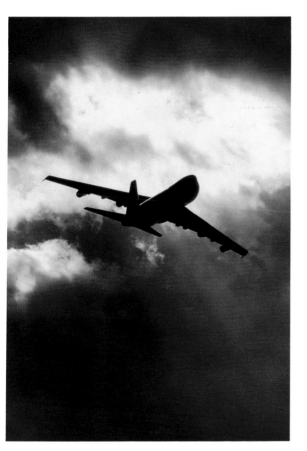

▲ A jumbo-jet in storm clouds is lit by nearby lightning flashes. If lightning should strike, it spreads harmlessly over the aircraft, although it may disturb the flight instruments.

Lightning Conductors

Lightning flashes do not always reach the ground. If they do, they head for tall objects sticking up from the surface, such as big trees or buildings. If lightning strikes a tree it may burst into flames. Lightning conductors prevent damage to tall buildings. These large strips of metal run between the topmost point and the ground. They give the lightning's energy a harmless route into the Earth.

Lightning flash

Lightning conductor (made of copper or similar metal)

Lightning conductor runs down side of building.

Energy of lightning spreads harmlessly into the ground.

All the Colors of . . .

A rainbow is one of the most surprising, beautiful yet fleeting parts of the weather. It is caused by the Sun shining on raindrops. Each drop of water acts as a tiny prism (see *opposite*) and splits the almost-white sunlight into its separate colors (see *below*). On a bright sunny day, you can make your own small rainbow with a hosepipe. Turn on the water for a powerful flow. Place your thumb over the end of the pipe to scatter the water into thousands of tiny drops. As the drops fall through the air, they act like rain and make a rainbow.

▶To see the rainbow, you must stand with your back to the Sun. The "rain-bow" is in fact a "rain-circle." You can only see part of it from the ground. People in an airplane can see the whole circle.

ROYGBIV

Sunlight is a mixture of different colors of light, which the rainbow shows as separate. The main seven colors are always in the same order. Red is on the outside of the arc, then Orange, Yellow, Green, Blue, Indigo, and Violet inside. Remember this by the historical saying: "Richard Of York Gained Battles In Vain."

The Heat Haze

On a hot day you might see a "heat haze." The Sun heats up the ground more quickly than the air. The hot ground warms the air just above it, which then rises, carrying dust and other small particles. The rising air and dust interfere with light waves, bending them as they pass through, to produce the shimmering effect. A dark road is a good place to look, since the dull tarmac surface heats up well (see *page 7*).

. . . The Rainbow!

A **prism** is a transparent object with angled sides, that bends the different colors in white light by different amounts. You can split sunlight to form a "long flat rainbow" by making a "long flat raindrop," using a mirror and water in a bowl.

Choose an open window in direct sunlight. Almost fill a bowl with clean water. Prop a piece of white cardboard upright, next to the bowl. Hold a mirror in the water (*right*). The curved water surface, where the water meets the glass, makes a prism that separates the colors in sunlight. Adjust the angle of the mirror to shine the rainbow on the cardboard.

▼ The Sun can, in hot places, produce heat hazes and even mirages. In a mirage, light rays from the sky reflect off the layer of very hot air near the ground, and then up into your eyes. It is like looking into a mirror and seeing a reflection of the sky. Because the image is blue and wavy with heat haze, it looks like water.

Window

Mirror

White cardboard

Weather Forecasts

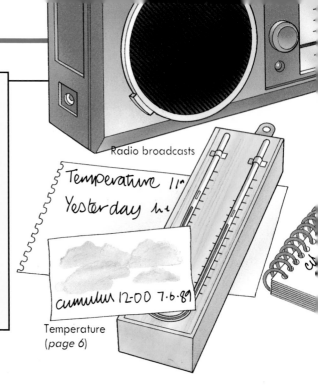

Radio broadcasts

Weather affects us all. On a sunny day, we can go outside. If it is raining, we'll probably stay indoors. Farmers plant their crops when the soil is moist, and harvest them when the weather is dry. If we know what the weather is likely to be we can make better plans. A whole branch of science, **meteorology**, is devoted to the study of weather.

Temperature
(*page 6*)

Your Own Weather Station

The various projects in this book show you how to build your own weather-measuring instruments and make weather records. On the right, you can see how to make a wind-strength recorder. It measures wind speed and direction at different heights above the ground (*see also page 15*). You can combine all your results in a Weather Notebook, along with information from the newspapers, radio, and television. Include atmospheric pressure readings (*see page 30*) from a **barometer**. Look for patterns in the weather. For example, does a sudden fall in temperature and an increase in wind speed mean rain is more likely?

Gathering the Information

Weather experts, or meteorologists, collect information from many sources, as shown here. They also obtain measurements from other countries, as part of the worldwide weather-recording network. The recordings from each place must be made in the same way, so that they can be compared and combined accurately.

The methods and measurements are agreed by the World Meteorological Organization (WMO). For example, wind speed varies with height. So the WMO has set a standard height of 10 meters (33 feet) above the ground, for recording winds. Much of the information is nowadays fed into powerful computers, which can look for patterns in the weather.

Weather stations

Weather balloons

Airplane reports

Weather ships

North

North West

7-6-89

Wind direction
(*pages 10 and 13*)

Rainfall gauge
(*page 20*)

Temporary knot

Wind speeds
(*page 15 and on the right*)

This kite-powered spring-balance compares wind speeds at different heights. Tie the balance to a peg by 5 feet of line. Launch the kite, and tie it by a temporary knot to the top of the balance. The strain indicates wind strength. Let out more line and see if it increases with height.

▶ The control center of a large meteorological center is packed with computers, display screens, and weather maps. Accurate forecasting of a big storm could save lives.

▶ A network of weather satellites, such as METEOSAT, send information down to ground stations.

Weather satellites

Weather aircraft

The Weather Map

Every day, the experts make weather forecasts that are given in the newspapers and on radio and television. Some people, like farmers and pilots listen to them regularly and are familiar with the special weather-words such as "**front**" and "**low**."

One of the clearest ways of showing what the weather is doing is to draw a weather map. But what do all the lines, squiggles, numbers, and arrows mean? Some of the main ones are described below. As you become more familiar with the words and symbols you can use your own weather observations to predict changes in the weather.

High pressure
The atmospheric air pressure (see page 4) varies with time, and from place to place. If it is higher than normal, this is called an area of high pressure or "high."

Low pressure
Places with lower than average atmospheric pressure are "lows." Pressure is measured in millibars (mbs). Standard atmospheric pressure at sea level is 1,013 mbs.

Isobar
On a map, contour lines join places of equal height above sea level. The lines (isobars) on the weather map join areas of equal atmospheric pressure.

Cold front
Here a region of cold air is moving against a region of warm air. The cold air, being denser, pushes under the warm air and makes it rise, and rain falls.

Warm front
This mass of warm air is pushing up against a region of cold air. The warm air is lighter and rises. Its water vapor condenses, forming clouds and rain.

Anticyclone
This is an area of high pressure, around which winds blow (see opposite). It often brings settled, fine weather. In winter the clear skies may mean frost.

The High Pressure System

"Highs" or anticyclones take up vast areas of the Earth's atmosphere and affect the weather across whole continents. The "high" is a region of high atmospheric pressure in which cool air sinks to the ground and then spreads out in the form of circling winds. The whole system may be thousands miles across and 10 miles in height.

In the Northern Hemisphere (the northern half of the world, above the Equator) the winds blow in a clockwise direction. In the Southern Hemisphere, they blow anti-clockwise. This is a result of the forces generated by the spinning Earth, in what is called the Coriolis Effect.

▶ The sinking air in the center of a "high" usually means clear skies, sunshine, and generally fine weather. This diagram shows a high pressure system in the Northern Hemisphere, where the winds spiral outward in a clockwise direction.

Cool air sinks toward ground

Area of high pressure in center

Winds blow outward and clockwise (in Northern Hemisphere).

The Low Pressure System

The "low," also called a "depression" or cyclone, is almost the reverse of the "high." Winds spiral inward, in an anti-clockwise direction in the Northern Hemisphere, and clockwise in the Southern Hemisphere. The air in the center rises, cooling as it does so. Cyclones in tropical areas may develop into hurricanes. Outside the tropics, they usually mean unsettled, wet, windy weather.

A typical "low" is 1,250 miles across and up to 8 miles in height. Cyclones tend to move and change faster than anticyclones. They are born, then grow and mature, and finally fade away and die, in some cases within a few days.

▶ As air rises in a cyclone, it cools in the upper atmosphere to form clouds, and often rain. Western Europe, and especially the British Isles, are often affected by cyclones moving eastward from the Atlantic Ocean, bringing strong winds and wet, blustery weather.

Clouds and rain often form.

Warm air rises from ground.

Area of low pressure in center

Winds blow inward and anti-clockwise (in Northern Hemisphere).

Weather Power

Every day, the land is under attack from the weather. Rocks are cracked by the Sun and by ice. Rain washes away loose soil. Rivers and glaciers rub great channels deep into the surface. The wind whips up waves that crash against the shoreline. These processes, known together as **weathering**, continually re-shape the landscape.

Make Your Own River!

Rivers are surface grooves along which water flows downhill. You can show how running water has the power to wear away, or erode, its banks. Place a layer of damp sand or soil on a large board, making a few "hills" and "valleys" in the landscape. Prop up one end of the board to make a shallow slope. Very slowly, trickle water from a pitcher onto the middle of the upper side. The water soon finds the quickest path down the slope. As it wears away a main channel, it carries away particles of sand or soil. This is erosion in action. (It is also why you should do this project outside!)

Water cuts away a "cliff" on the outside of each bend.

A New Course

Over hundreds and thousands of years, huge land movements buckle and tilt the Earth's surface. Copy this by tilting the board slightly, to see how your "river" finds a new course.

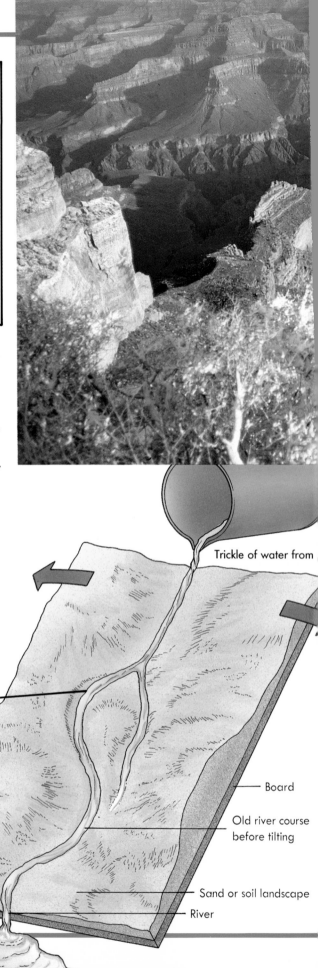

Trickle of water from

Board

Old river course before tilting

Sand or soil landscape

River

Sculpted in Stone

Over thousands of years, the forces of the weather can reduce the hardest of stone to dust. But the Earth's surface is made of many different rocks, some tougher than others. The softer rocks are worn away faster, leaving the hard ones. In Monument Valley, Arizona, hot sunshine and sand-blasting winds have rubbed away the softer rock to reveal harder "stumps" of stone. To the west, the Colorado River (*left*) has cut the gigantic Grand Canyon deep into the Earth.

The Power of Ice

Water, like air, becomes more dense and contracts as it cools (see page 5). But when its temperature goes below about 39°F. it begins to expand again and get bigger. As the water freezes into ice it continues to expand—and almost nothing can stop it.

Ice that forms in plumbing pipes may split them open. When the temperature rises and a thaw sets in, the ice melts, and the water floods out! This is why, in cold weather, it is important to wrap (lag) water pipes and protect them from the freezing temperatures.

▼ Fill an empty plastic ice-cream or margarine container with water, right to the brim. Clip on the lid, and place it in a freezer or icebox. As the water freezes into ice, it expands and pushes off the lid.

After freezing, the lid is pushed off by ice power.

Fill container to brim with clean water.

Ice cream or magarine container

33

Weather and Climate

Weather shapes the physical world of rocks and running water. It also affects the living world—the types of plants and animals in each area. However, the word "weather" applies to conditions in a small area, such as a county or state, and over a short time, during days or weeks. The word **climate** is used for whole countries and continents, and during long time periods, from years to many centuries. The world can be divided into several "climate zones" (see page 37). In the tropics around the Equator, the climate is warm all year round, and daylight is very nearly 12 hours each day. At the North and South Poles, it is bitterly cold, and there is continuous daylight for half the year and darkness for the other half.

Climate zones going up a mountain are similar to those going "up the world" from the tropics to the North Pole (see page 37). Mountain zones are narrower. Temperatures fall by 1°F. for every 280 feet above sea level.

Mountain Climate Zones

1 Permanent ice and snow on the summit.
2 Alpine scrub, with cold winters and short summers.
3 Montane forest, often damp from cloud and rain.
4 Tropical forests need both high temperature and rainfall.
5 Tropical grasslands form in warm but drier regions.

1 Mountain ibex

2 Hedgehog

3 Tiger

4 Orangutan

5 Elephant

34

Houses Against the Weather

Probably the most widespread animal in the world is the human. People can live almost anywhere, from the tropics to the poles, because they build dwellings that shield them from the weather. The dwellings differ from one region to another, depending on local conditions such as the temperature, rainfall, and wind, and also the local building materials. In addition, history and tradition shape our houses.

In the pine forests of the cold, snowy north, there are plenty of trees available. A common design is the log cabin (*right, above*). Its thick walls keep wind and snow out, and keep heat in.

The Tuaregs of the Sahara build tents of thin poles and animal skins (*right, middle*). The wide roof gives good shade, and open doors allow a cooling breeze. A "typical English cottage" (*right, bottom*) has a roof thatched from locally grown reeds, small windows, and timber-framed or stone walls. It is cool in summer and warm in winter.

Log cabin

Nomad tent

How a house's heat is lost

25%

Roof

Windows

10%

Walls

35%

Draft gaps

und

15%

15%

Thatched cottage

Today's Typical House

Many modern houses have been built to a standard square-box design. This makes a house easier and cheaper to build, but means that traditional dwellings with "local character" are disappearing.

◀ In the past few years, we have realized that it is vital to save energy, especially from "fossil fuels" such as coal, oil, and natural gas. A typical house loses heat energy in many ways (*left*). We can cut down the waste by better building methods and materials, along with extra insulation.

Nature and the Weather

Seaweed   Fir cone

In natural wild places, plants and animals live in harmony with the weather and the seasons. With the warmth and moisture of spring, seeds begin to grow. Animals feed on the growing plants and begin to raise their young. In summer, the plants flower. Bees, birds, and other creatures spread the flower pollen, helping to form seeds. In the fall seeds and fruits ripen, while animals feed well and make stores for the winter. In winter many plants and animals go to "sleep" until spring.

Gardeners must look after plants, weeding and watering, protecting them from animals, and perhaps raising them in a greenhouse. Left on their own, these "unnatural" plants usually die, and the natural plants and animals take over.

Many plants use the weather, and especially the wind, to spread their seeds. Dandelion and thistle "parachutes" float on the slightest breeze. Ash seeds, or "keys," twirl away from the tall parent tree on their "wings." The wind shakes the seeds from ripe poppy capsules. As lupin pods dry out they suddenly snap open and fling their seeds away. A piece of seaweed absorbs moisture from humid air and becomes flexible and rubbery rather than stiff and dry. Fir cones open their scales in dry weather, to release the seeds within.

Dandelion seeds

Thistle seeds

Ash seeds

Lupin seeds

Poppy seeds

Weather Folklore

Many local sayings and legends are based on the weather. In Britain, July 15 is St Swithin's Day. It is said that if it rains on this day, it will rain for 40 days. Statistics show that the myth is not really true. In the U.S.A., February 2 is Groundhog Day. It is said that the groundhog wakes up from winter sleep and looks outside its burrow. If it sees its own shadow, the weather is fine — but cold, so the groundhog goes back to sleep for six more weeks.

Animals Around the World

Wild creatures of the world cannot live anywhere. A gorilla could not survive in the icy wastes of Antarctica. An Arctic hare would not live long in a tropical forest. Each kind of animal is suited only to a certain climate. The climate has direct effects on the animal itself, by its temperature, humidity, rainfall, and winds. It also has effects on the surrounding animals and plants, which provide food and shelter for others, and which are all tied into the natural network of life.

The broad wildlife zones across the world are known as "biomes," and they resemble the different zones as you travel up a mountain (see page 34). However, some animals have been able to "cheat" nature and spread to unsuitable areas—but only with our help. Farm animals such as sheep, cattle, goats, and pigs are fed and housed by us in places where they could not otherwise survive. Cats, dogs, and other pets rely on us for food and shelter. More unwelcome guests like rats and mice survive almost anywhere that we do.

▼ The diagram below shows the main climate zones from the Equator to the North Pole, and examples of animals from each zone. There are similar zones toward the South Pole.

ARCTIC
NORTHERN TEMPERATE
NORTHERN SUBTROPICAL
TROPICAL EQUATORIAL
TROPICAL EQUATORIAL
SOUTHERN SUBTROPICAL
SOUTHERN TEMPERATE
ANTARCTIC

Polar bear

Arctic hare

Brown (grizzly) bear

Badger

Snake

Gorilla

ARCTIC

TEMPERATE

SUBTROPICAL

EQUATORIAL

EQUATOR

A Change in the Weather?

The Earth's climate has changed many times in the past. Subtropical forests have spread from the south into temperate areas. Millions of years later, ice sheets have spread from the north. Today, the great danger is that we are changing the climate. Can Earth survive?

The Greenhouse Effect

In bright sunshine, the air inside a greenhouse becomes warm. The greenhouse glass lets in the Sun's light energy and some of its heat energy. Inside, part of this energy is "reflected" and converted into a different type, which cannot pass back out through the glass so easily. The energy, in the form of heat, builds up inside the greenhouse.

You can show this with two identical glass jars, each containing cold water. Wrap one in a plastic bag (this is the greenhouse "glass"). Leave them in the Sun for an hour. Then measure the temperature of the water in each jar (above). Which is warmer?

Clear plastic bag around jar

Jar of water

Thermometer measures water temperature.

The same thing is now happening to the Earth. Over the past few centuries, people have been burning fuels such as wood, coal, oil, natural gas, and gasoline, in ever-increasing amounts. The gases formed by the burning, such as carbon dioxide, are building up in the atmosphere. They act like greenhouse glass. The result: experts believe the Earth will heat up and undergo "**global warming**."

◄ ▲ Burning large areas of forest speeds the Greenhouse Effect. As the Earth warms, the oceans will expand and polar icecaps will melt. The rise in sea level could flood many major cities (*above*).

Acid Rain

The weather can transport pollution across seas and continents. Power plants (*right*), factory chimneys and vehicle exhausts pour all manner of chemicals into the atmosphere. They include sulfur dioxide and nitrous oxides. These react with substances already in the atmosphere, and with water, to form weak acids. The polluted clouds and air float for hundreds of miles on the wind.   Eventually the acidic moisture falls to Earth as rain—acid rain. The acids damage trees, rivers, and

▲ Power stations are one of the main sources of fumes that make acid rain.

lakes, killing fish and other water creatures. They even eat away statues and the stonework of buildings.

Acidic fumes from factories and cars

Polluted air is blown hundreds of miles.

Pollution falls back to the surface as acid rain.

The Ozone Hole, and How We Can All Help

Many of today's products could alter our climate in the future. Recently, experts discovered that certain chemicals in aerosols and refrigerator cooling fluids are entering the atmosphere and damaging the **ozone layer**. This layer of ozone gas, high in the atmosphere, filters out much of the

Refrigerator

Aerosols

Sun's harmful rays. If the layer becomes thinner or disappears, damaging rays would reach the surface. They could cause many problems, such as an increase in skin cancers.
    Manufacturers are now making "ozone-friendly" aerosols to help reduce the risks.

◀ This computer-colored satellite photo shows the thinning of the ozone layer over Antarctica, in late 1988. The developing "hole" is colored in blue.

Index

Page numbers in *italics* refer to illustrations, or where illustrations and text occur on the same page.

Editor: Thomas Keegan
Designer: Ben White
Illustrators: Kuo Kang Chen
                  Peter Bull
Consultant: Terry Cash

Cover Design: Pinpoin Design Company
Picture Research: Elaine Willis

Photographic Acknowledgments
The publishers would like to thank the following for kindly supplying photographs for this book:
Page 4 Courtesy, Philips; 5 Science Photo Library; 6 Quadrant Picture Library; 8 Science Photo Library; 9 Mary Evans Picture Library (top left) Supersport (bottom left) Science Photo Library (top & bottom right); 10 ZEFA; 12 Science Photo Library; 15 Spectrum Colour Library (left) Science Photo Library (right); 18 Science Photo Library (top) ZEFA (bottom); 20 Science Photo Library (left top & bottom) Courtesy, BOC (right); 22 ZEFA; 24 Science Photo Library; 27 Science Photo Library; 28 Courtesy, Everyready; 29 ZEFA; 32 Science Photo Library; 36 Science Photo Library; 37 N.H.P.A. (top) Science Photo Library (bottom); 38 Friends of the Earth (top) Greenpeace Communications (bottom); 39 Science Photo Library.

Published in 1990 by Warwick Press,
387 Park Avenue South, New York, N.Y. 10016.
First published in 1990 by Kingfisher Books.
Copyright © Grisewood and Dempsey Ltd. 1990

Library of Congress Cataloging-in-Publication Data

Parker, Steve.
   Weather/Steve R. Parker.
      p.   cm.—(Fun with science)
   Summary: Suggests experiments and projects illustrating basic principles and phenomena of meteorology, including precipitation, temperature, wind, and seasonal changes.
      ISBN 0–531–19086–2
1. Weather—Juvenile literature. [1. Weather—Experiments. 2. Experiments.] I. Title. II. Series.
QC981.3.P37   1990
551.5—dc20   90–12029
                                         CIP
                                         AC